Practical Solutions

to Everyday Challenges
for Children with
Asperger Syndrome

Practical Solutions

to Everyday Challenges
for Children with
Asperger Syndrome

Haley Morgan Myles

Foreword by
Jeanie McAfee, M.D.

© 2002 by Autism Asperger Publishing Co.
P.O. Box 23173
Shawnee Mission, Kansas 66283-0173

Publisher's Cataloging-in-Publication
(provided by Quality Books, Inc.)

Myles, Haley Morgan.
    Practical solutions to everyday challenges for children with Asperger Syndrome / Haley Morgan Myles. social difficulties. — 1st ed.
    p. cm.
    SUMMARY: Self-help book for children with Asperger's. syndrome from a child's point of view.
    Audience: Ages 5-11.
    Library of Congress Control Number: 2002114208
    ISBN: 1-931282-15-3

    1. Asperger's syndrome—Handbooks, manuals, etc.— Juvenile literature.
2. Asperger's syndrome—Patients— Juvenile literature. (1. Asperger's syndrome—Handbooks, manuals, etc.) I. Title.

    RJ506.A9M95 2002   616.89'82
                                QBI33-789

This book is designed in Mook and Tekton

Managing Editor: Kirsten McBride
Cover Design and Illustrations: Eddy Mora
Design and Production: Eddy Mora and Tappan Design
Photography: Stephen Locke Portraits

Printed in the United States of America

I dedicate this book to my mom, my dad,

and all of the people who helped me with this book:

Kirsten McBride, Linda Schwartz, the American Girl authors,

and Monica Nugent. Most of all, I would like to thank

the kids who helped me learn about Asperger Syndrome.

FOREWORD

I have had the great pleasure of spending several days with Haley Morgan Myles at one of the many conferences she attends with her parents, Brenda Smith Myles and Keith Myles. I was immediately struck by her poise, intelligence, and sunny disposition. Throughout her childhood, Haley has been steeped in the subject of autism and Asperger Syndrome. Her mother, Dr. Brenda Smith Myles, writes and speaks internationally on autism and Asperger Syndrome and is the director of the only graduate education program in the United States that currently offers a master's degree in Asperger Syndrome. Haley has been involved in her parents' work, treated as a part of the team from the time she was old enough to voice her own thoughts. And voice her thoughts she does in this book, and she does it well! *Practical Solutions* is chock full of Haley's ideas about handling a myriad common and not-so-common challenges that may confront a young person with Asperger Syndrome.

Although Haley wrote *Practical Solutions* for children with Asperger Syndrome, parents and teachers will find that the child-to-child format and down-to-earth advice make it a good read for other youngsters as well. Each challenge and suggested set of solutions is presented in a short, easy-to-read paragraph. Haley has included sections on challenges at school, getting along with others, dealing with emotions, safety tips, first aid, and more. She covers a rich variety of topics, ranging from learning how to do something you don't enjoy doing, to what to do if you can't find something you are looking for. (Many of us adults will find the latter topic helpful too!) Some of Haley's suggestions are tried-and-true solutions that our grandmothers taught us as children. Others are Haley originals. In both cases, these refreshingly simple and well-written ideas will prove enormously helpful to young people of all types.

Jeanie McAfee, M.D.
Author, *Navigating the Social World*
November, 2002

Hello fellow kids!

I wrote this book for kids like you who may have a
hard time with things that happen every day. This
book might help you get along a little bit better.
My mom is a presenter. She teaches parents and
teachers about Asperger Syndrome and I have
learned a little about Asperger Syndrome from her.
I have also learned about Asperger Syndrome from
kids I know with Asperger Syndrome. Whenever my
mom goes to a conference, I often go with her
and get to meet and play with kids with Asperger
Syndrome. We usually have a great time! I've also
met some kids with Asperger Syndrome at Camp
Determination where I have been a camper. This is
how I got interested in Asperger Syndrome and
made this book.

– Haley M. Myles

TABLE OF CONTENTS

SCHOOL-RELATED

GETTING ALONG

EMOTIONS AND CONCERNS

OFFICER DAVE'S SAFETY TIPS

FIRST AID

MISCELLANEOUS

SCHOOL-RELATED

1 TESTS

Everyone takes tests. Sometimes you might worry when you have to take a test. Study, focus and, on the day of the test, eat a good breakfast. Scientists have discovered that students who eat a good breakfast do better at school. If you get nervous when the test is given to you, say to yourself, "I can do this!" Take a deep breath before you start. If you can't think of an answer to a problem, skip it and come back to it later.

If you have a hard time writing, ask the teacher if you can use a computer to type the answers or if you can tell the teacher the answers without having to write them down.

2 MAKING HOMEWORK EASIER AND FUN

To get some variety and maybe even learn better and faster, change the way you do homework sometimes. Do your homework using a gel pen instead of a pencil, or type your answers using a computer. You can also invent new ways to make games out of learning! For example, instead of doing flashcards the old way, try to play "Go Fish" with a friend. You can play "Go Fish" to learn addition, subtraction, multiplication, or division. If you are learning to add, you can ask your partner for 3+2, and your partner will give you a card with the number 5 on it. You can check your answer with a calculator.

You can also take turns playing games and working; for example, you can work for 15 minutes and then play for about 10 minutes. It is best to do the work you don't want to do first instead of worrying about it. Just try to think about doing it in a different way. I love inventing new things. How about trying your ideas soon?

3 ASKING QUESTIONS IN CLASS

If you want to ask a question at school, raise your hand. If the teacher doesn't come to you after a bit, walk up to the teacher and say, "Excuse me, I have a question." If the teacher still doesn't answer, say it again louder. If you can't explain the question clearly, write it down on a sheet of paper and ask yourself if you understand the question yourself. If not, try writing the question again in different words. If rewriting the question isn't working, do something else for a couple of minutes to take your mind off it and try again.

4 REDOING WORK THAT YOU GOT A BAD GRADE ON

If you get an assignment back from your teacher with a bad grade on it and your teacher tells you to redo it, ask the teacher if there is an easier way for her to explain how to do the assignment, or ask her to show you again how to do the problem. The teacher will probably say yes. Learn how to do it, and BINGO you have it!

If you don't like to ask the teacher for help, think about what will happen. You will probably get a bad grade again because you still don't understand what to do. If you have a choice between discussing the problem with your teacher and getting a bad grade, what do you think you should do? Talk to the teacher! There you go!

5 LEARNING HOW TO DO SOMETHING YOU DON'T ENJOY

There are many things you can do for this problem. Try to make a game for each thing that you don't like to do. Here are two examples: If you don't like taking a bath, put a toy in the bathtub, like a rubber ducky. If you don't like to brush your teeth, try a new flavor of toothpaste or an electrical toothbrush, etc., etc.

6 REMEMBERING THINGS

It is sometimes hard to remember things. Here are some ideas that you can try to help. Write the things you can't remember on a little card and put it in a place where you will see it each day. Pretty soon you will probably have memorized it.

If you cannot write, ask your parents to remind you what you are supposed to do at the proper time. For example, if you need to remember to wash your face before you go to bed, your parents can say, "Did you remember to wash your face?" just when you are about to go to bed.

You could also draw a picture to remind yourself. To remember to put lotion on your face before you go to bed, you could draw a figure of a soap man. His body would be a bar of soap and he would be holding a bottle of lotion. You could tape this to the mirror in the bathroom where you wash your face. If you can't remember to raise your hand in school, you can draw a little guy raising his hand or get a bendable figure who is raising her hand and leave it on your desk. If you get a bendable figure, it is probably not a good idea to mess with it while you are doing your work.

You can also do something fun to help you remember! Pretend that you can predict things! Every day, a person comes in to see you who is forgetful. Tell the person the text on the card without reading it. If you are able to do it correctly, go on and try to remember another one!

7 IF YOU FORGET YOUR SCHOOL LUNCH

If you are at school and forgot to pack your lunch, here are some solutions. Tell your teacher or the school secretary and ask them what to do. Usually, they will let you have a free lunch and you can pay them back the next day.

8 HAVING PROBLEMS DOING YOUR HOMEWORK

If you are doing your homework and can't figure out the answer to a problem, do something else for a couple of minutes. This will help you relax, and it sometimes helps you remember what you are supposed to do. If that still does not work, ask your parents or older brother or sister to help you.

9 IF YOU NEED HELP WITH SCHOOLWORK WHEN THE TEACHER IS BUSY WITH SOMEONE ELSE

If you need help and the teacher is with someone else, like another student or a teacher, skip the problem you are having difficulty with and go to the next one. If it is okay with your teacher, ask your neighbor to help you. If you can't ask a neighbor, skip the problem and raise your hand to get help from the teacher. Do not get upset if you have to wait for a little while. If the teacher finishes with the other student or teacher and does not see that you have your hand raised, you can say, "Excuse me, can I have some help?"

10 FOLLOWING DIRECTIONS

If you don't understand instructions on how to do something, ask the person to explain it an easier way. If it still doesn't help, ask him if he could write it down on a piece of paper.

For example, if you don't understand directions at school, ask your teacher if she can explain it an easier way, such as writing it down on the blackboard or showing you an example. If she is with someone else, don't forget to raise your hand to get help. It is okay if you don't understand as long as you ask for help.

GETTING ALONG

1 LISTENING

If someone is talking, it is polite to listen. If you look at the person who is talking, he or she will know that you are listening. If someone talks for a long time about a subject that you are tired of, or not interested in, you can say, "Excuse me, can I talk now, please?" or "Can we talk about something else?"

2 HOW TO DRESS FOR SPECIAL OCCASIONS

If you are going to a party or other special occasion and don't know what to wear, ask your parents or a friend who will be there too what she/he is wearing. It is important to be clean and to try to look your best.

3 IF YOU BREAK SOMETHING BY ACCIDENT

If you break something, some parents want you to tell them right away. Other parents may want you to clean up the mess before you tell them. You know best what the agreement is in your family. Always apologize for breaking the item.

If you break something at someone else's house, tell the person, say you are sorry and offer to help clean up the mess. To show how sorry you are, you might offer to replace the item you broke.

4 IF THINGS ARE NOT RETURNED IN TIME

If you let somebody borrow something and they don't return it, ask if you can get your object back. If the person thinks that he had it only for a little while, think about it. Maybe he had the item only for three days or so. If that is not the case, tell your mom and dad about it. They can probably help.

If you get an object returned, such as a stuffed animal or a favorite sweatshirt, and it is dirty, tell the person who borrowed it in a polite way to clean it. If they still return it dirty, don't let them borrow your stuff again. If someone borrows something such as a baseball card or an American Girl card and ruins it, do not loan them anything again until they pay for the damaged item.

5 KEEPING PROMISES

Sometimes, it is hard to keep promises. Here are some tips on keeping promises. (1) Do not make promises quickly. (2) Before you make a promise, think about it. Will it be hard to keep? Can you do it? (3) If someone else makes a promise and breaks it for a special reason, forgive them. For example, if your dad promises to take you camping, and on the day of the camping trip he breaks his arm and can't take you, that is not really breaking a promise. Your dad cannot help it.

6 HOW TO HANDLE SOMEONE WHO BRAGS AND SHOWS OFF

If someone shows off, ignore it. For example, if your friend says, "Look at how many trophies I have. I have more than anyone," say, "That's nice" and try to talk about something else.

Some people like to talk about themselves all the time like, "I won last year's race. I won this year's race. I have millions of trophies and I just won a race now." If the bragging gets worse, talk to your parents or your teacher. They usually have good advice. If they don't have any helpful suggestions, try to ignore the irritating behavior or stay away from the person, if possible. If you like the person and would like to stay friends, you might just need to tell him that he is talking about himself a little too much and that bragging is not nice. Tell him that there are other things to talk about and give him a few examples.

7 FORGIVING A FRIEND

If your friend is angry with you and you don't know what you did or said wrong, think about it. Pretend that you are your friend, and think about what you said. Would you be happy if someone said that to you? Do you now feel sorry? If not, here is another idea. You can try writing a note to your friend explaining what happened and maybe say you are sorry.

If you are angry with a friend because of something she did, tell your friend how you feel. If you cannot do that, try to write about something you like. That should keep your mind off her. If that does not work and you are still angry, it is time to ask your parents for advice.

I told my friend, Abby, that I didn't like the way Lily always bragged about herself. Abby told Lily and I felt bad because (1) I was telling Abby a secret and she did not keep the secret and (2) I didn't want to hurt Lily's feelings even though I didn't like her bragging. I was angry with Abby for a little bit, but then I forgave her. I also thought that I probably should not be saying something about Lily that might be a little mean.

8 PROPER TELEPHONE BEHAVIOR

• HOW TO START A PHONE CONVERSATION

If you are talking to a person you know, start out by saying, "Hi, this is (your name)." Then you can ask, "How are you doing?" or "What is going on?" If the person on the other end can't think of anything to say, it is your turn to talk! Talk about something that is going on at your house or maybe about a TV show you have seen, a new toy, etc., etc.

• HOME ALONE

If the phone rings when you are home alone and you and your parents have decided that it is okay for you to answer it, ask who is calling and tell them that your mom or dad is not available to come to the phone right now. Do not say that your mom or dad is not home. Don't forget to get the person's telephone number and take a message. It is best if you repeat back the name, phone number, and what the person wanted before you hang up.

If your family has an answering machine, sometimes it is a good idea just to let incoming calls go to the answering machine when you are home alone.

• OBSCENE PHONE CALLS

If you ever hear an obscene phone call, hang up immediately. Write what time the person called and what he or she said. If there's more than one call, do this every single time. Tell your parents or another adult immediately.

• ANSWERING MACHINE

If you call somebody and get an answering machine, be sure to speak especially clearly and slowly. Leave your first and last name, the name of the person you want to reach and your telephone number.

9 WHAT TO DO IF YOU ARE AT A PARTY AND DON'T KNOW ANYONE THERE

If you are at a party, Scouts or anywhere else and do not know anyone, look for someone who you think it would be nice and interesting to meet, or look for somebody who also seems to be alone. Walk up to that person and say "Hi!" If the person seems to ignore you, say "Hi!" again, but louder. If the person still does not answer, try to find someone else to talk to. Say, "Hi!" and tell the person your name. Ask them questions about their interests, pets, etc. Tell jokes, talk about the latest musical group, etc., etc.

10 HOW TO INTRODUCE SOMEBODY

When you need to introduce someone to a friend or relative, introduce the oldest person first. For example, if John is your uncle and Mary is your friend, say, "Uncle John, this is my friend, Mary. Mary, this is my Uncle John."

11 HOW TO MAKE YOUR FRIEND COMFORTABLE

If your friend is new to your house, show him around. If your friend is staying for a while, ask if he wants a drink or a snack if you know that's okay with your parents. Take turns playing games with each other. Have fun!

12 BEING RESPECTFUL

Be respectful because it makes other people feel good. It also might make you feel good. Here are some ways that I have learned to be respectful: (1) listen to people when they are talking, looking directly at them and not interrupting; (2) say "please" and "thank you"; (3) treat other people's things as special as you would treat your own things; (4) don't brag or show off; and (5) say nice things. If you have a guest over, being respectful means that you ask them what they would like to do first. Then you can do what you want second.

13 FOLLOWING RULES

Follow the rules so you don't get into trouble. Sometimes you may not like a rule that your teacher or parents set. If you don't like the rule, ask them if you can compromise. If it is impossible to compromise, try to follow the rule even if it is hard. You usually get used to following the rule eventually.

Most parents make rules to keep you safe. Sometimes it is hard for kids to understand that. When you get to be a parent, you will probably have the same type of rules for your kids and your kids will probably not like the rules either.

14 KNOWING WHAT TO TOUCH AND NOT TOUCH

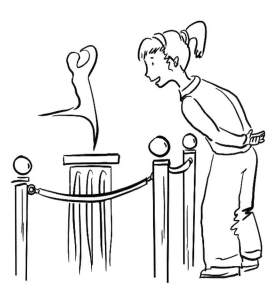

Sometimes it is hard to know what to touch or not to touch when you see something interesting in a shop, in somebody's house, etc. Here are a couple of solutions. Pretend that you own the thing that you want to touch so badly. Would you let someone touch it? If you think so, you can probably touch it. If not, don't touch it. If you are still not sure, here are a couple of other ideas. If there is glass covering the item, do not touch it! If there is a rope in front of it, as there sometimes is in museums and stores, don't touch it! If you are still in doubt, ask someone you trust.

15 HOW TO START A CONVERSATION

If it is a person you don't know, start out saying, "Hi, my name is (add your name)." Talk about a popular band, the weather, jokes, etc. If you know the person, say, "Hey, (add the other person's name)" and talk about things that you both enjoy and already know about each other.

16 IF YOU RECEIVE A GIFT YOU DON'T CARE FOR

Thank the person who gave it to you, even if you don't care for the gift. You can always exchange it, or never use or wear it. Say, "Thank you very much for the (name of the gift)" and add something nice about the gift, such as, "Pink is one of my favorite colors." Never tell the person that you don't like the gift. It would hurt their feelings. If it's an item of clothing, wear it when you invite the person over who gave you the gift.

17 IF YOU RECEIVE A PRESENT THAT YOU ALREADY HAVE

If you get a gift you already have, you can exchange it for something else. Thank the person for the gift. Do not make any bad faces or say anything impolite. If you think about it, the gift was the perfect gift. The person thought you would like it — and you do. You just already have it. You can say, "Thank you very much for (name of gift)" or "I really like the (name of gift)."

18 SPILLS

If you spill something, tell an adult that you are sorry and try to clean it up. Do not get upset. It is okay if you spill a little. Everyone spills something once in a while.

19 GOING TO A WEDDING

If you are invited to a wedding, talk to your parents about what to wear — something that is comfortable but fancy is best. Be quiet during the ceremony. When the bride throws the bouquet of flowers, if you are a girl, you may want to jump, but don't wrestle with others to get it. If the guests dance after the wedding, you can dance too! Have fun!

Sometimes there is a place at the party where kids can hang out if they are bored with toys, electronics and more. If you get bored and you don't have anything to do, be patient and remind yourself that the wedding will soon be over.

20 FORMAL PARTIES

If you are going to a formal party, talk to your parents about what to wear — something that is comfortable but fancy usually works best. Be very polite (see tips for LISTENING). If you are introducing someone, say the older person's name first. For example, say, "Uncle Bob, this is Lily. Lily, this is Uncle Bob." Bring a book or a small toy along so you won't get bored.

EMOTIONS AND CONCERNS

1 WORRYING ABOUT THINGS YOU SHOULDN'T BE WORRYING ABOUT

If you are worrying about things that you shouldn't be worrying about, don't think about the future, because you never know what will happen. There are a lot of things that you should not worry about because they might not happen: (1) tornadoes, (2) hurricanes, (3) fire, (4) getting a bad grade on a test, (5) getting a disease, (6) not being first in line, or (7) spilling your milk during lunch.

Try to think about happy things, not sad things. Instead of worrying about not being first in line to go to lunch, think of the good things that you will eat at lunch. Instead of worrying about getting a bad grade on a test, think about how proud you are of yourself that you will do your best.

2 FEARS

Everyone is afraid of something: the dark, missing the bus, make-believe creatures, etc. Ask your mom and dad what they were scared of when they were your age. Ask how they conquered their fears. It could help you.

3 HOMESICK

If you are at a friend's house and miss your parents, tell your friend's parents that you want to go home. Then call your parents and ask them to come and pick you up. Sometimes when you feel homesick, just talking to your parents will make you feel better, so you may not want to leave. Either way, it's okay.

4 FEELINGS

Share your feelings, but not too much or too little. For example, it is okay to say, "I am really upset because (say what you are upset about)" so that people will know how you feel. It is probably not okay to say that three or four times in a row or have a tantrum. If you don't share your feelings, you may feel as if you have a hole in your stomach, and that hurts a lot. On the other hand, if you share your feelings too much, it may bore others. It is important to share your feelings with your family.

5 GETTING UPSET

If you feel like you are going to scream or yell, go to your room and punch your pillow, listen to music, draw or do something else to calm down. If you get upset at school and feel like you are going to yell, tell your teacher that you would like to leave the classroom to calm down. Maybe you can go to the bathroom or take a short walk.

6 AFRAID OF THUNDERSTORMS

Don't be afraid of thunderstorms. If you like music, pretend that the rain is a drum, that the wind is a broken flute, etc. If you like sports, pretend a ball is hitting a bat when you hear thunder. If you like mechanics, pretend that the sounds you are hearing come from an old, noisy factory. Soon it will be fun listening to thunderstorms.

7 BEING EXCITED

If you are so excited about something special that is about to happen that you can't think of anything else, here are a couple of solutions to help take it off your mind: (1) Try to keep your mind off of it by keeping busy and doing something you like. (2) Set a timer or alarm that will go off when the special event is going to happen. That way, you don't have to think about it in the meantime. (3) Ask your parents to let you know when the exciting thing is close to happening so that you can do something else fun while you are waiting. (4) Write in your diary about it. Sometimes writing in a diary can help you understand how you feel and become calm or feel better. (5) Ask your parents for other ideas.

8 IF SOMEONE HURTS YOUR FEELINGS

If someone hurts your feelings, it is probably just an accident. But if it happens several times, tell your teacher or your parents and ask them what to do. If your parents' advice does not help, try to stay away from the person who is hurtful. Sometimes kids say things to hurt others' feelings because they don't feel good about themselves. It is hard to remember that when someone is calling you a name or teasing, so the safest thing is to stay away.

9 WHAT TO DO WHEN YOU'RE ANGRY, SAD, OR YOUR FEELINGS HAVE BEEN HURT

If you are angry or sad about something, talk with your mom or dad about it because they can usually help. If you are angry, it is usually not appropriate to scream, yell or hit. Try to relax, think about something else, go to your room and punch your pillow, or anything else that can make you feel better. You usually will need to talk it over with the person who made you angry or sad, but make sure that you know what you want to say first. Don't say anything to hurt the other person's feelings; that won't help. You can practice what to say with your parents first.

OFFICER DAVE'S SAFETY TIPS

Not everybody is as lucky as I to have an uncle who is a police officer. In this part I would like to share some of his advice for staying safe in many different kinds of emergencies or difficult situations.

1 CALLING "911"

Call "911" if there is an emergency. After you dial "911" and someone answers, say your first and last name, where you live, or where the emergency happened, your phone number, and what is wrong. Speak slowly and clearly so the operator can understand and take the necessary action to send help.

2 SMELLING SMOKE

If you ever smell smoke or dangerous fumes, tell everyone in the house. You need to have an escape plan to get out of the house. If your family does not already have a plan, suggest that you sit down and develop one. You might also want to get a carbon monoxide detector that will help detect dangerous fumes.

See also FIRE

3 FIRE

If you smell smoke or there's a fire in your house, it is important that you and your family get out as soon as possible. If you are in your bedroom with the door closed, do not open it. Put the back of your hand on the door knob. If it is hot, do not open the door.

Go to another door or go to the nearest window to get out safely. When you open the window, do not jump if there is nothing soft to land on. If there is a tree nearby, climb down it as quickly as possible. If you are on the second floor and there is an elevator, do not go on the elevator. Go down the stairs. If you cannot do any of these things, yell and scream for help out of the window. If the door knob is cold, open the door and crawl to the nearest exit (door or window). Get out as fast as you can. Do not go back in the house to get anything. Nothing is as important as your life. You can always get another book or toy later on if your things are damaged or lost in a fire.

Make sure your fire alarm is working. It is good to check it every week. My uncle says, "Tuesday is test day." Change the battery every year on a day that you can remember like your birthday or January 1.

4 DRUGS

If you find something that looks like drugs, pills, a syringe, etc., tell your teacher, parent or an adult you trust immediately. Do not pick up, eat, or touch anything. If someone offers you drugs, say "No!" immediately, run away from the person, and tell an adult you trust what happened.

5 CAR SAFETY

Make sure you always wear your seatbelt in the car. That way, if you are in an accident, you are less likely to get hurt. If you are under the age of twelve years old, always ride in the back seat because the air bags in the front could hurt you badly if you are in an accident. Always lock the doors.

6 LEAKS AND BROKEN WATER PIPES

If you notice water leaking from a pipe or faucet in your house, tell your mom or dad immediately because they may need to call a plumber, or try to fix it themselves. If you don't like the sound of a faucet dripping, put a small towel or washcloth in the sink so you can't hear the sound, but make sure the water can still drain out.

7 ELECTRICAL SPARKS

If you notice a spark from an electrical outlet or appliance, turn the appliance off. Do not unplug it. Tell an adult immediately. If a fire begins, see FIRE for what to do.

8 IF THE LIGHTS GO OUT

If the power goes out in part of the house, your family may have too many electrical appliances plugged in at the same time, such as toaster, microwave, TV, computer, air conditioner, etc. Do not tug on any cords because you might hurt yourself. If they haven't already noticed, tell your parents or another adult that the lights are out. They may have to put in a new fuse or reset the fuse box. If your whole neighborhood does not have electricity, it is probably a power outage, and the power company will have to fix it. If you are without power for a long period of time, you may have to stay with friends or relatives or in a hotel.

I always keep a flashlight in my nightstand and we also have one in the kitchen.

9 DANGEROUS ANIMAL

Some animals that do not look dangerous may actually be dangerous. For example, a snake might look harmless but it could bite you. A mouse is small but it might carry diseases. Do not touch the animal or go near it. Tell an adult you trust about it instead and ask for help.

A good rule is not to touch an animal that is not yours unless you have permission by the owner. Do not touch wild animals unless they are in a petting zoo.

10 TORNADO

If a tornado hits your area, it is recommended that you get food and water and go to low ground, like a basement. If you do not have a basement, go to a bathroom in your house or a place that has no windows. Getting under a table is also a safe thing to do. Put cushions on you to protect yourself from falling glass or anything else that might cause damage to your body.

If you are in a car and a tornado is coming, get out of the car with the adult and go to a deep ditch and lie down flat. Stay as close to the ground as possible. It is not safe to go in a car if you hear that a tornado is coming.

11 HURRICANE

If a hurricane hits, do not panic. Your family probably has a safety plan; if not, you may suggest that they develop one for the future. It is recommended that you get food, water and a raincoat. Go to high ground. You can also go to a hurricane shelter if there is one near you.

12 BROKEN GLASS

If you ever see broken glass, do not walk in it or touch it. If you break something and there is glass all over the floor, tell your parents or another adult. Be very careful when cleaning up, as tiny pieces of glass can be hard to see but can cut you badly. Sometimes your parents might not want you to clean up the pieces because they think you might get hurt. If that is the rule in your house, wait for your parents to clean up the broken glass and stay away from the area in the meantime.

13 GUNS

If you ever see a gun, do not mess with it! If someone is playing with it, tell the person to stop and immediately leave the area. If they ask why, say, "It is a weapon and can kill people." If they still do not stop, tell an adult you trust about it. Even if they do stop, you still need to tell an adult you trust!

14 KNIVES

If you ever see a person playing with a knife, tell them not to do it. If they ask why, tell them that knives are sharp. If they do not stop, leave the area, and talk to an adult you trust. Never play with knives, and be careful using them. If you are cooking and need to use a knife, be very careful and make sure you know how to use knives. If you are a beginner, it is best to start with a safety knife that can cut food, but not people. My mom bought me a safety knife so I could learn to cut and cook. Be safe!

15 IF SOMEONE IS IN A FIGHT

If kids are fighting with each other, tell them to stop. You probably don't want to jump in the middle of the fight because you might get hurt. Get help from an adult immediately. If you hear someone saying that they are going to be fighting later on, tell an adult. Ask the adult not to tell the kids that you said anything, because you don't want to get the reputation of being a tattle-tale.

16 STAYING AWAY FROM STRANGERS

If you are ever approached by a stranger in the street who wants you to go with him or her or wants you to help find a puppy in a store or any place else, don't respond but start running in the opposite direction. If there's somebody else nearby, go up to them and ask for help or call out. Tell your parents or other adult about the stranger and ask for advice. You can always ask a police officer for help.

17 IF SOMEONE KNOCKS ON THE DOOR WHILE YOU ARE HOME ALONE

You and your parents probably have a rule about opening the door, especially when you are at home alone. If it is okay to open the door for certain people, it is a good idea to have a list of their names. If someone knocks on the door and you are the only one home, DO NOT open the door if the person's name is not on the list, even if you know the person. Look through the peephole. If you know who it is, write the person's name on a piece of paper so you can remember who came to the door and tell your parents later on.

18 BULLIES

Get away from anybody who is teasing or bullying you or your friends. If it is at school, tell your teacher or playground supervisor. If it happens after school, go in the opposite direction and be sure to tell your mom or dad exactly what happened when you get home. You can also ask a police officer about safety tips to deal with bullies. If bullies want money, candy or anything else, do not give it to them. If you do, they will probably pick on you again.

19 IF YOU ARE STUCK IN AN ELEVATOR

If you get stuck in an elevator, don't panic. There is usually an emergency phone or a red button to push in the elevator. Lift the phone and call, or push the red button. If there is neither of these, yell out loud. People will hear you.

FIRST AID

See CALLING "911"

1 IF YOU GET A CUT

If you get a regular, everyday cut or scrape, rinse it with warm water and put a Band-Aid on it. If it is a bad and deep cut, tell your mom, dad or other adult. If necessary, they will take you to the emergency room or call "911" for an ambulance.

2 SICK PET

If you think your pet is sick, tell your parents or another adult. Let your pet rest, and put his food and water bowls by his bed. Call the veterinarian and ask for tips or medicines to cure your pet. Follow your veterinarian's advice and check your pet every couple of minutes to see how he is doing.

3 SPLINTER

If you get a splinter, tell an adult. The adult will probably numb it with ice and try to pull it out with a pair of tweezers. If it hurts too much when you put the tweezers on it, you and your parents might decide to let it fall out by itself. Watch to make sure that the area does not get infected by cleaning it carefully and maybe putting some medication on it. An adult can help you do this.

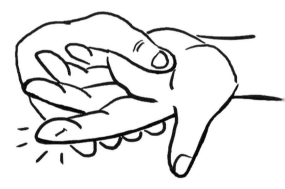

4 BITES

If chiggers bite you, don't panic. Ask an adult for some medication to stop the itch, and don't make it worse by scratching. If you have no medication available, clear fingernail polish or cortisone cream usually works. Sometimes soaking in an oatmeal bath can also stop the itching. But regardless of what you try, be sure to ask an adult for help.

If a dog or some other animal bites you and breaks the skin, tell your parents or another adult immediately. Ask the person who owns the animal if it has had a rabies shot. If not, or if there is no owner around, you need to see your doctor as soon as possible to get checked out and possibly get a tetanus shot. If the animal bite does not break through the skin, there is usually nothing to worry about. Anyway, always tell your parents and wash the area carefully.

5 BROKEN BONES

If you ever see someone and you think he has broken a bone, tell an adult as the person will need to go to the doctor or the emergency room. If there is no adult around, call "911." If you get hurt yourself and think you have a broken bone, stay where you are and call out for an adult to find you. Be prepared to go to a hospital for x-rays and other treatment.

6 CHOKING

If you are ever choking, make the universal sign for choking, or if you are able to talk, tell others around you that you are choking. If someone else is choking, yell out and get an adult as quickly as possible to do the Heimlich maneuver. This is a special way to help people who are choking; to do the Heimlich maneuver a person has to be specially trained.

7 IF YOU LOSE A TOOTH

If your tooth falls out, wash your mouth out with water, if possible. If you want to save your tooth, clean it and get a small plastic bag, if available, to put it in. Let your parents know that you lost a tooth.

If one of your teeth is knocked out, immediately tell an adult as you will probably have to go to the dentist. If possible, save the tooth and take it with you to the dentist.

8 INFECTION

If you think you have an infection, tell your mom or dad, so they can arrange a doctor's appointment, if necessary. An infection can be a rash or red bumps that irritate your skin, a sore with a red circle around it, or a sore with pus coming out.

9 NOSE BLEED

If you ever have a nosebleed, don't panic. It happens to most people at one time or another. To help stop the bleeding, hold your head high in the air and pinch the very top part of your nose. Wash the blood away. Make sure you find your parents, teacher or other adult and tell them your nose is bleeding.

10 IF YOUR FEET HURT

If your feet hurt, tell your parents to take a look. Your shoes may be too small, your shoes might not be built right for your feet, or maybe you have a bruise. Keep your toenails cut square because if you don't, you might get an ingrown toenail, and that can make your feet hurt too.

11 INJURED ANIMAL

If you come across an injured animal, don't push or touch it. Stay away, because injured animals will run or fight if someone gets too close. If an adult is with you, one of you should call the owner or Animal Control.

12 STINGS

If a wasp stings you, tell an adult. The adult will usually find some kind of medicine, spray or cream that can make it feel better. If you are allergic to bees or wasps, find an adult immediately. You may have to go to the doctor and get a special prescription.

13 WHAT TO DO IF YOU FIND SOMEONE WHO IS HURT

If you find someone who is hurt, ask if she is all right. If the person has a skinned knee or elbow, help her get up and take her somewhere to get the area washed and get a Band-Aid. If you don't know what to do, comfort the person until help arrives. If it looks like a serious injury, never try to move the person as it could make the injury even worse.

MISCELLANEOUS

1 GETTING LOST IN A STORE

If you get separated from your family in a store, go to the checkout register and ask for help. Tell the cashier your family member's or other adult's name, and describe what he or she looks like. Some families have a certain spot they go to when they are lost. My friend Ivy and her family always go to the back right-hand corner of the store and wait for each other if one of them gets lost. It is important not to panic and not to go with anyone who is not your family member. The only exception would be to ask a person who works in the store for help.

2 SHARING THINGS WITH YOUR BROTHER OR SISTER

Try not to fight or argue about toys, games, or other things. If you have something that is very important to you, ask your mom and dad if it is necessary to share it with others. If they tell you to share, tell your brother or sister that you want to play with your toy first for at least 10 minutes, and then they can use it for 10 minutes after that. You might want to set a timer to keep track of the time to make sure it's fair.

3 WANTING TO STAY UP LATE

If you want to stay up late, it is best to do it on Fridays and Saturdays so you won't get too tired on school days. If you want to stay up late on school days, ask your parents for permission. If it's okay, set your alarm clock so you can wake up on time in the morning.

4 IF YOU ARE LOCKED OUT OF YOUR HOUSE

If you have an automatic garage door opener, make sure you know the code. The code is usually something that is easy to remember by everybody in your family, such as a holiday or somebody's birthday. Keep a piece of paper with the code on it in your backpack to help you remember but make sure the note doesn't say "garage door code." You might also want to talk to your parents about giving a key to your neighbor so you can go to the neighbor's house and borrow it if you are locked out. Remember to return the key for future use.

5 IF YOU CAN'T FIND SOMETHING YOU ARE LOOKING FOR

If you cannot find something you are looking for, remain calm. Try to think of the last place you had the item. If you start to get upset, think about something else and do something else for about 10 minutes. Then try to look for it again. You may want to ask an adult, brother, sister or friend to help you look. Also, if you put things in their correct place when you are done with them, you probably will not have this problem very often.

6 IF YOU GET HUNGRY

If you get hungry, fix yourself something simple. Follow the rules your family has for what appliances you can use if an adult isn't home and what foods you can eat. Eating cereal is almost always a good idea, especially when you can't think of anything else.

7 HOME ALONE

If you are home alone, make sure you have all of the necessary phone numbers (business, cell phone, etc.) so you can get ahold of your parents or other adult in case you need them. Try not to think about your parents too often because that might make you feel sad. Play games, be safe, and have fun! You might also want to call a friend on the telephone, if it is okay with your parents. Do not invite anyone over unless you have permission to do so. Keep your doors locked.

8 IF YOU ARE LONESOME

If you are lonely, ask your parents if you can call one of your friends. If you are still lonely after hanging up the phone, ask your parents if one of your friends can come over and play. If they say no, ask if your parents or other family members want to play a board game with you, or swing, read a book, etc., etc. Have fun!

9 HOW TO KEEP YOURSELF BUSY IN A CAR OR ON AN AIRPLANE

Plan ahead for your trip. Choose small things like a coloring book and crayons, a Walkman with CDs and headphones, books, travel-size games, crossword puzzles, and magazines to pack in a backpack or small suitcase that you can take with you. If your parent brings a laptop computer, you can ask if you may use it. You can use the laptop with music CDs, DVDs, and computer games. My mom usually buys me one or two small things that I have not played with before so I can have something to do on the trip.

10 IF YOUR PET GETS LOST

If your pet is lost, tell your mom or dad as soon as possible. Also call the animal pound to let them know. Tell them where you live, your phone number, and your pet's name. You might also want to make a poster about your pet and put it up in your neighborhood. If possible, the poster should have a picture of your pet, a description of your pet, your pet's name, directions for what to do if someone finds your pet, and your phone number. In most cases, pets are soon found.

11 PICKING UP YOUR TOYS

If you don't pick your toys off the floor, the "toy fairy" may come and take them away in the middle of the night. You, or somebody else, also might trip over the toys and get hurt, or you may forget where your toys are the next time you want to play with them. If you don't always want to pick up your toys immediately after you have played with them, ask your parents if there is a place where you can leave them out for a while. I have a little playroom where I can leave things out for a while. No matter what, it is best to clean up your toys every day because if you don't, it becomes a big mess and then it takes even longer to clean up.

12 IF YOU FIND SOMETHING THAT DOES NOT BELONG TO YOU

If you find something that doesn't belong to you, take it to the nearest Lost and Found if you are in a store or somewhere like that. If you find something on the street, ask the person closest to you if he or she lost something. All you need to say is, "Did you lose anything?" You don't want to give all of the details about the item. If the person answers yes, ask him or her to describe what the lost item is to be sure this is the rightful owner.

13 BEDWETTING

If you happen to wet your bed, don't worry. Many kids have this problem. Avoid drinking liquids late in the day and go to the bathroom right before you go to bed. If you do wet the bed, tell your mom or dad immediately so they can help you put on clean sheets and covers.

14 TROUBLE FINDING THINGS OR BEING ORGANIZED

If you lose a worksheet, ask the teacher for another one. Do not get upset. Try to put things away in the same place each time you use them. Sometimes a special notebook, like Intelligear, can help you organize your schoolwork.

I have baskets in my bedroom. Each one is for a certain type of toy or book. I put my hair things in one basket and my Password Journal in another. I keep most of my Egyptian stuff on one shelf so I know where it is.

15 SOMETHING BOTHERS YOUR SENSES

If you are outside and the sun is too bright, go inside or wear sunglasses. If you are inside and the light is too bright, ask your teacher or parents if you can turn out the lights and open the shades.

If it is too warm and you are wearing a sweater, take off the sweater. If you are still too warm, ask your teacher or parents to lower the temperature.

33

If a sound is hurting your ears, you might want to wear earplugs. Ask your parents if you can carry earplugs with you wherever you go if a lot of sounds bother yo

If you are a picky eater, make sure that you have something you like to eat. I am a picky eater and I always have a snack with me just in case someone wants me to eat a food I don't like.

16 SOMEONE ASKS YOU TO DO SOMETHING MEAN OR BAD

If someone asks you to do something mean or bad to someone else, say "No, it wrong to hurt kids or hurt their feelings." Someone who asks you to do something wror is not a friend because friends would not do that to each other.